SPOT 50
Trees

Camilla de la Bedoyere

Miles Kelly

First published in 2010 by Miles Kelly Publishing Ltd
Harding's Barn, Bardfield End Green, Thaxted, Essex, CM6 3PX, UK

This edition printed in 2013

2 4 6 8 10 9 7 5 3

Publishing Director Belinda Gallagher

Creative Director Jo Cowan

Editors Carly Blake, Sarah Parkin

Image Manager Liberty Newton

Production Manager Elizabeth Collins

Reprographics Stephan Davis, Jennifer Hunt

Assets Lorraine King

ISBN 978-1-84810-604-8

Printed in China

British Library Cataloguing-in-Publication Data
A catalogue record for this book is available from the British Library

ACKNOWLEDGEMENTS
The publishers would like to thank the artist Vivien Wilson who has contributed to this book

The publishers would like to thank the following sources for the use of their photographs:
Colin Varndell 7(l), 10(l), 15(l), 16(l), 17(l), 19(r), 34(m), 37(m), 41(b), 43(m), 45(r), 50(m), 52(r)
FLPA 34(r) Roger Wilmshurst **Shutterstock** 39(t) Richard Griffin, 42(bl) joanna wnuk, 45(l) Kletr,
47(t) dabjola **Still Pictures** 27(r) D.Harms/WILDLIFE

All other images are from the Miles Kelly Archives and WTPL

With thanks to the Woodland Trust for their
valuable contribution to this book

Made with paper from a sustainable forest

www.mileskelly.net   info@mileskelly.net

CONTENTS

Tick the circles when you have spotted the species.

SEASON WATCH

Each season brings with it different natural events and changes to trees that you can look out for, such as leaves changing colour in autumn and flowers opening in summer. For fun things to do all year round visit naturedetectives.org.uk

Spring

Trees that have been bare all winter come to life in spring. From late February to early March, leaf buds start to grow. With little else to eat, birds search for leftover seeds and insects on and around trees. By April, leaves are opening and flowers are blooming. By May, oaks, horse chestnuts and hawthorns are in full flower.

Summer

By June, many flowering trees are in full bloom. Butterflies, such as red admirals and peacocks, can be seen visiting flowers in hedgerows and woodland. Elder flowers bloom, producing a strong, sweet scent. Oaks are having a second growth spurt and new stems and leaves can be seen on the tips of their branches.

Autumn

As trees change in preparation for winter, their leaves turn a glorious array of browns, oranges and reds. Fruits ripen, attracting animals and birds. Once oak leaves have fallen, look for 'oak apples', or galls, on the tree. These are parts of the tree – buds, leaves or roots – that have swollen because insects have laid their eggs inside them.

Winter

By winter, deciduous trees have lost their leaves. Squirrels and birds still visit them in search of fallen fruits, or to reach their nests. Small mammals, such as hedgehogs, often hibernate in the piles of leaves around a tree's base. At winter's end, male hazel catkins release clouds of yellow pollen to fertilize the small, red female flowers.

PARTS OF A TREE

Trees have one tall, thick, woody stem called a trunk. The trunk is at least 10 cm thick, and it allows the tree to stand up by itself. Most trees have a distinct crown of leaves and reach more than 4 m in height. Like trees, shrubs are woody plants, but they don't reach great heights and have more than one stem.

Flowers are the first stage in producing fruit. They must be pollinated before they can develop

Leaves absorb carbon dioxide and take in sunlight, and release oxygen. This process, called photosynthesis, creates the plant's food of sugars

Fruits contain seeds that are released when the fruit dries up, rots, or is opened by animals

Tiny hairs grow along the outside of a plant's root, which help the plant to absorb water and minerals from the soil

Tiny tubes called xylem carry water from the roots around a plant. Other tubes, called phloem, carry energy-rich sap

Leaf shape

Leaves come in many shapes and sizes but there are two main types – needle-shaped leaves and broad leaves. Features to look for are not only the overall shape, but also: the number of leaflets on the same stalk, whether leaflets are paired or offset and whether the edges are 'toothed'. The five leaf shapes below relate to the five sections in this book.

Oval

Long

Compound

Hand-shaped

Needle

ALDER ALNUS GLUTINOSA

The wood of the alder is fascinating – when it is submerged in water, it becomes as hard as stone. Much of the Italian city of Venice is built on piles of alder wood, which were sunk into the sand banks. Houses and other buildings were then built on top. The small, winged seeds of this water-loving tree get carried along by streams and rivers to grow further downstream. It is said that the green dye of the alder flower was used to colour the clothes of Robin Hood.

DECIDUOUS

FACT FILE

Height 18–25 m

Where Widespread; woodland, hedgerows, often near water

Flowering February/March

Fruiting October–December

Leaf tint/fall November

Rounded with toothed edges

Side buds are on short stalks

Shiny and dark green in colour

Smaller female catkins develop into cones (fruit)

Male catkins (flowers) are up to 5 cm long

Mature cones are woody and open to release seeds

ASPEN
POPULUS TREMULA

Fluttering leaves, which tremble in the breeze, give the aspen its Latin name *tremula* and its common name of 'quaking aspen'. The autumn-dry leaves of the aspen produce a rustling noise even in gentle breezes. Herbalists once used its flowers to treat people suffering from anxiety or nightmares. In Medieval times, the timber was used to make houses for the poor who could not afford oak.

DECIDUOUS

Male and female catkins (flowers) grow on separate trees

FACT FILE

Height 15–25 m

Where Widespread; hillsides, hedgerows, often near water

Flowering March

Fruiting May

Leaf tint/fall October

Buds have pointed tips

Male catkins are reddish purple and up to 8 cm long

Green female catkins develop into seed capsules (fruit) that contain many hairy seeds

In summer, new leaves emerge coppery brown, turning to green

Rounded or slightly oval

Tiny, fluffy seeds are easily carried in the wind

BEECH FAGUS SYLVATICA

Beech trees have long been part of Britain's history, especially in the furniture-making industry. Particularly grand trees have been called 'queen beeches', and impressive beech woods are known as 'nature's cathedrals'. Since Roman times, beech wood was used for fuel and it was preferred for making furniture for its pink-orange colouring. Its nuts – called mast – were used as feed for animals.

DECIDUOUS

FACT FILE

Height 10–35 m

Where Southern and eastern England, South Wales; woodland, chalky or sandy soils

Flowering April/May

Fruiting September–November

Leaf tint/fall November–April

Female flowers are green and spiky on short stems

Male flowers hang on long stems

Long, narrow buds

One or two nuts are held in a prickly four-lobed casing (fruit)

Triangular, shiny, brown nuts are called mast

Pointed tip

Glossy and dark green

BLACK POPLAR POPULUS NIGRA

Once common along riverbanks, today the native black poplar is very rare and found only in southern England and parts of Ireland. Only a few hundred female black poplar trees exist in Britain and few of them grow near males. This means that seeds are rarely produced, so new trees are hard to find. Arrows found on the wreck of the *Mary Rose* were made of black poplar wood – they had survived 400 years under the sea.

DECIDUOUS

FACT FILE

Height 20–25 m

Where Southern England, Ireland; often near water

Flowering March/April

Fruiting April/May

Leaf tint/fall October

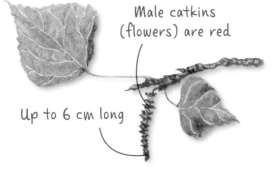

Male catkins (flowers) are red

Up to 6 cm long

Green female catkins develop into seed capsules (fruit)

Fine tooth on edge

Seed capsules contain brown, cottony seeds

Smooth and tan coloured

Can range from diamond to triangular in shape

BLACKTHORN PRUNUS SPINOSA

This deciduous tree is distinctive because its flowers are some of the first to appear in spring, appearing even before its leaves. The fruits of the blackthorn are known as sloes and, although bitter to taste, they are popular with birds. It has long been considered a magical tree. In Celtic mythology it was home to fairies, and a blackthorn staff (long stick) was thought to be ideal for keeping evil spirits away.

DECIDUOUS

FACT FILE

Height 6–7 m
Where Widespread; woodland, scrubland, hedgerows
Flowering March/April
Fruiting August/September
Leaf tint/fall October/November

Sharply pointed, stiff spines

Fruits are blue-black berries, called sloes

Tiny, white, scented flowers have five petals and emerge before the leaves

Dull green, 2 to 4 cm long

Dark, almost black in colour, and spiny

Finely toothed edge

BOX BUXUS SEMPERVIRENS

Slow-growing and never gaining great height, box is considered to be more of a shrub than a tree. Its small, glossy, evergreen leaves grow tightly together, making it a perfect plant for garden hedges. Box can be cut and shaped into ornamental bushes in a practice known as topiary. It has an unpleasant smell, which caused Queen Anne (1665–1714) to have it removed from the gardens of Hampton Court Palace. Although common in gardens, box is rare in the wild.

EVERGREEN

FACT FILE

Height 6–8 m

Where Southern England; gardens, chalky soils

Flowering January–May

Fruiting August–September

Leaf tint/fall Evergreen

Male and female flowers grow together in clusters

Male flowers are yellow, female flowers are greenish

1.5 to 3 cm long on hairy twigs

Small, tough and glossy

Three-horned, woody seed capsules (fruit) are up to 8 mm long

Seed capsules open to release several black seeds

BUCKTHORN RHAMNUS CATHARTICA

In the past, plants and trees were used to treat illnesses and buckthorn is no exception. The ripe, black berries are mildly poisonous to humans, but they are a source of food for many birds. When herbal remedies were common, a tea made from buckthorn berries was used to treat a stomach ache, even though it causes vomiting and diarrhoea! The bark of a young tree is orange-brown and darkens with age.

DECIDUOUS

FACT FILE

Height 4–6 m

Where Widespread; hedgerows, woodland

Flowering May/June

Fruiting September/October

Leaf tint/fall October/November

Flowers grow in clusters

Sharp thorn at tip

Small, yellow, four-petalled flowers are scented

Pointed tip

Fruits are berries that contain two to four seeds each

Shiny, black berries are up to 8 mm long

Dark and glossy with a smooth surface

COMMON LIME TILIA X EUROPAEA (VULGARIS)

The widely planted common lime is easy to spot as its leaves, and anything under them, get covered in a sticky substance called honeydew. Tiny insects called aphids suck sap (a sugary liquid) from the tree and produce honeydew. This attracts dirt, and by autumn, the leaves are sticky and filthy and so are cars that may be parked beneath its branches. Beekeepers often place their hives near lime trees so that the bees produce 'lime honey'.

DECIDUOUS

FACT FILE

Height 20–40 m

Where Widespread; woodland, parks, gardens, streets

Flowering July

Fruiting September

Leaf tint/fall October–November

Red buds

Groups of small, scented, yellow, five-petalled flowers hang on long stalks

5 to 10 cm long with a pointed tip

An extra leaflet, called a bract, helps the fruits to travel in the wind

Small, hard, round fruits

Look at the back of the leaf — if it has small clumps of red hairs at the base of the veins, it could be a small-leaved lime

Slightly heart-shaped with tufts of hair on the underside

CRAB APPLE MALUS SYLVESTRIS

Crab apples have been cultivated (grown especially) for hundreds of years, but a truly wild tree can be told apart by its thorns. These trees produce small, sour apples that are not good to eat raw, but they are often made into tasty crab apple jellies and jams. Crab apple wood is hard, heavy and strong, making it ideal for items that endure heavy wear, such as tools. The wood produces a pleasant smell when burnt.

DECIDUOUS

FACT FILE

Height 7–9 m

Where Widespread, except Scotland; woodland, hedgerows

Flowering April/May

Fruiting September/October

Leaf tint/fall October/November

Petals are white with pink tinges

Flowers are up to 4 cm across and grow in clusters

Toothed edges and a pointed tip

Young fruits are yellow-green, and rosy-red and green when ripe

The small apples grow up to 4 cm in diameter

Long stalk

Reddish-brown with small buds (wild trees also have thorns)

DOGWOOD CORNUS SANGUINEA

This small tree or shrub has red stems that are especially noticeable in winter when there are few colours to brighten the dark days. Dogwood has nothing to do with dogs. The wood is hard and was once used to make skewers known as 'dags'. This gave the tree its old name of dagswood. The leaves of dogwood can be identified by gently pulling them apart – stringy latex can be seen where the veins have been broken.

DECIDUOUS

FACT FILE

Height 2–5 m

Where Widespread; woodland, scrubland, hedgerows

Flowering May/June

Fruiting September–November

Leaf tint/fall October/November

Small, white, bad-smelling flowers grow in clusters

Flowers have four petals and are up to 1 cm across

Reddish in colour

Smooth edges and deep veins with a pointed tip

Fruits are black, pea-sized berries

Berries are bitter to taste and not good to eat

Leaves turn dark red in autumn

ENGLISH ELM ULMUS PROCERA

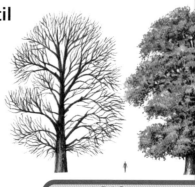

English elms were common in Britain, until the onset of Dutch elm disease killed 25 million of them in the 1970s. It is thought that this tree was introduced to Britain 2000 years ago by the Romans, and some scientific research suggests that all English elms descended from just one tree. This meant that many elms were equally vulnerable to disease. Today, elms can often be seen growing in hedgerows.

DECIDUOUS

Purple flowers are in small clusters

Flowers appear before the leaves

FACT FILE

Height 16–30 m

Where Widespread; woodland, hedgerows

Flowering February/March

Fruiting April–June

Leaf tint/fall October/November

Fruits are on short stalks

Toothed edges

Papery, winged fruits contain one seed each

Thick and reddish in colour

One side is longer than the other, similar to the wych elm

GOAT WILLOW SALIX CAPREA

The goat willow is also known as 'pussy willow' because its springtime male catkins are soft and grey – like a cat's paw. Goat willows are important trees in woodland and hedgerows because they are linked with many types of butterfly and moth. Some larvae feed on the leaves and others live under the bark. As the male catkins mature and turn yellow they are called 'goslings' because they are the same colour as baby geese.

DECIDUOUS

FACT FILE

Height 4–10 m

Where Widespread; woodland, hedgerows

Flowering March/April

Fruiting May

Leaf tint/fall October/November

Grey at first, turning to yellow

Male catkins (flowers) are up to 10 cm long and silky to touch

Male and female catkins appear on different trees

Buds are green with a reddish tint

Female catkins (flowers) are green and longer than males

Long and oval

Upright seed capsules (fruit) hold lots of silky, hairy seeds

Dull green, and slightly hairy on upper surface

HAZEL CORYLUS AVELLANA

As hazel catkins turn yellow it's a sign that spring is coming, and when squirrels start to gather hazelnuts winter is just around the corner. Hazels are not only a source of food for many types of wildlife, but they provide home and shelter for them too. They often grow in dense clusters with lots of stems growing from the ground, rather than a single trunk.

DECIDUOUS

Fruits are smooth, round, woody nuts

Nuts sit in ragged, green or brown, leafy husks

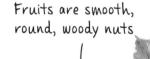

FACT FILE

Height 12–15 m

Where Widespread; woodland, scrubland, hedgerows

Flowering February

Fruiting August/September

Leaf tint/fall November

Toothed edges and slightly hairy

Stiff hairs and small, oval buds

Female flowers look like buds with tiny, red tassels

Short stalk

Long, drooping male catkins (flowers), known as 'lambs' tails'

18

HORNBEAM
CARPINUS BETULUS

The statuesque hornbeam is an impressive deciduous tree with its pale silvery-grey bark, and yellow-green catkins in the spring. It's often coppiced (stems cut back to the ground causing many long shoots to grow) or pollarded (top branches cut) and it is commonly planted for hedging. The white wood is very fine-grained, which makes particularly good firewood and charcoal. The Romans made their chariots from the wood because of its strength.

DECIDUOUS

FACT FILE

Height 10–20 m

Where Southern and eastern England; woodland, hedgerows

Flowering March

Fruiting September

Leaf tint/fall November–April

Male catkins (flowers) are yellow-green with red specks

Green female catkins develop into fruits

Fruits are tough nuts with a three-lobed leaflet, or bract, attached

Long buds

Pointed tip

Double-toothed edge

MULBERRY MORUS NIGRA

The black mulberry tree has a long history rooted in Southeast Asia where it has been cultivated for thousands of years. It was introduced to Europe by the Romans, who dedicated the tree to Minerva, goddess of Wisdom. It has been widely planted and is grown in sheltered gardens for its delicious fruits, which contain a staining dye. It is celebrated in the nursery rhyme, 'Here we go round the mulberry bush'.

DECIDUOUS

Green female flowers are 1 to 2 cm long

FACT FILE

Height 8–10 m

Where England; mostly gardens

Flowering May

Fruiting July

Leaf tint/fall October/November

Male flowers are yellow-green and longer than the female flowers

Rough to touch on upper side

Fruits are sweet when ripe

Raspberry-like fruits are purple-red when ripe

Buds are broad and pointed

Toothed edges

PEAR PYRUS COMMUNIS

The pear tree originally came from Southwest Asia, but is now common throughout Europe. Pears have undergone many changes since they first arrived in Europe as farmers have cultivated sweeter and juicier varieties of the fruit. Pear trees can be found in gardens and orchards in Britain, especially southern areas. The wild pear, which is a different type, is rare, and its fruits are hard, gritty and smaller than those of the *Pyrus communis*.

DECIDUOUS

FACT FILE

Height 9–15 m
Where Southern England; orchards, woodland, gardens
Flowering March/April
Fruiting September/October
Leaf tint/fall November

Flowers have five pure-white petals

Centres are pink-purple

Reddish-brown and hairy when young

Pointed tip

Pears ripen to yellow-green, sometimes slightly rosy

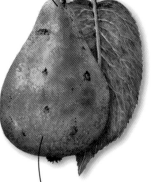

Fruits are hard pears up to 12 cm long

Smooth or finely toothed edge, up to 8 cm long

PLUM PRUNUS DOMESTICA

Plum trees are most commonly found growing in orchards and gardens. Plums were probably created as a hybrid (mix) of blackthorn and cherry plum. Today, plums are the second most cultivated fruit in the world. The plum *Prunus domestica* is first mentioned in 479 BC in the writings of the Chinese philosopher Confucius – it is listed as a popular food in Chinese culture. A tree will not produce fruit until it is four or five years old.

DECIDUOUS

FACT FILE

Height 8–10 m

Where Mainly England; orchards, gardens

Flowering April/May

Fruiting July–September

Leaf tint/fall October/November

Clusters of flowers

Smooth and brown

Flowers are all-white, sometimes tinged with green

Finely toothed edges

Smooth skin

Purple fruits are large, round and juicy

Upper surface is smooth and lower surface has tiny hairs

SILVER BIRCH — BETULA PENDULA

With its silvery bark and fluttering leaves, the silver birch is sometimes called 'Queen of the forest'. It was one of the first trees to start growing in Britain at the end of the Ice Age, around 10,000 years ago. It is known as a pioneer species, which means it is one of the first plants to grow in a new area. Silver birch produces huge crops of seeds of up to one million every year. This tree is easily recognizable by its silver-grey bark, even in the winter.

DECIDUOUS

FACT FILE

Height 18–25 m

Where Widespread; woodland, scrubland

Flowering April–May

Fruiting June

Leaf tint/fall November

Brown, with small bumps, or warts

Winged seeds are 1 to 2 mm long and are released from the fruits

Slender, green female catkins (flowers) develop into seed capsules (fruit)

Male catkins are long, drooping and yellow

Double-toothed edges

WAYFARING TREE VIBURNUM LANTANA

Once common alongside footpaths in southern England, the wayfaring tree grows in hedgerows, scrubland or on chalky ground. Today, it is a more common sight in gardens, grown for its ornamental leaves, large flower heads and bright berries. Despite their attractive appearance, the berries are mildly poisonous and should not be eaten. The young and flexible stems can be used to make twine.

DECIDUOUS

Flowers have five petals

White flowers appear in dense clusters

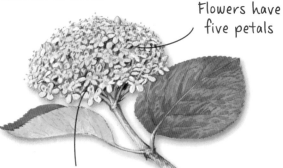

FACT FILE

Height Up to 6 m

Where South England, south Wales; hedgerows, scrubland, chalky soils

Flowering May

Fruiting August/September

Leaf tint/fall October/November

Underside is hairy

Rough upper surface with deep veins

Grey-brown and hairy

Fruits are oval berries that turn black when ripe

Berries are up to 8 mm long

WHITEBEAM
SORBUS ARIA

When the leaves of the whitebeam first open in the spring they appear white, giving this tree its name ('beam' is the Saxon word for tree). The whiteness is caused by the young leaves' soft coating of white hairs. Hair on the topside soon disappears as the leaves mature and droop downwards, but the undersides stay white. The wood of the whitebeam is very hard-wearing, and its small, red fruits can be made into jam and wine.

DECIDUOUS

FACT FILE

Height 8–15 m

Where Southern England; woodland, chalky soils

Flowering May/June

Fruiting September

Leaf tint/fall October/November

Green buds

White hairs on the underside

White flowers grow in loose clusters

Each berry contains two seeds

Fruits are oval-shaped berries that turn red when ripe

Up to 8 cm long

WILD CHERRY
PRUNUS AVIUM

When its branches are laden with white flowers or bunches of glossy fruits, the wild cherry attracts many birds. According to folklore, this tree has particular associations with cuckoos. The birds are believed to need three good meals of cherries before they will stop singing. The wood of a cherry tree is fine-grained and a beautiful shade of red, making it popular with cabinet makers.

DECIDUOUS

White, five-petalled flowers grow in groups of up to six

FACT FILE

Height 18–25 m
Where Widespread; parks, woodland
Flowering April/May
Fruiting July/August
Leaf tint/fall October/November

Berry-like fruits ripen to red

Long, pointed tip

Brownish red buds

Up to 15 cm long with toothed edges

26

WILD PRIVET
LIGUSTRUM VULGARE

For centuries, gardeners have taken wild trees and shrubs, such as privet, and grown them as ornamental plants. Privet is one of a few trees and shrubs that is described as being semi-evergreen. Depending on climate, it may or may not lose its leaves in winter. Privet is commonly grown in gardens, cut neatly into hedges, but the wild form looks very different, with long branches that reach upwards. The flowers and fruits were once used to treat eye and mouth diseases despite being poisonous.

SEMI-EVERGREEN

FACT FILE

Height 3–5 m

Where Southern and central England, Wales; gardens, streets, parks

Flowering May/June

Fruiting September/October

Leaf tint/fall Semi-evergreen

Flowers grow in cone-shaped clusters

Cream-coloured, sweet-scented flowers attract insects

Small and shiny

Flowers develop into fruits

Fruits are shiny, black berries

Young twigs are covered in short hairs

WYCH ELM ULMUS GLABRA

In Middle English (a language spoken long ago) the word 'wych' meant bendy. Wych elm trees are not particularly bendy, but their young shoots are and they can be bent and twisted for making into baskets and other goods. These trees were badly affected by Dutch elm disease – a fungus carried by a wood-boring beetle. The leaves of the Wych elm are the largest of any native tree and can be up to 18 cm long!

DECIDUOUS

FACT FILE

Height 16–30 m

Where Widespread; hedgerows, woodland

Flowering February/March

Fruiting May/June

Leaf tint/fall October/November

Flat, winged fruits are 2 cm long and contain one seed each

Purplish flowers grow in clusters

Covered in stiff hairs when young

Uneven base, similar to the English elm

Twelve to eighteen pairs of veins, more than the English elm

HOLLY ILIX AQUIFOLIUM

With its clusters of red berries and prickly leaves, the holly tree is steeped in myth and mystery and is the subject of many superstitions. Although it was thought that cutting holly would bring bad luck, the custom of bringing holly into the home at midwinter goes back thousands of years. Hanging holly was thought to ward off evil spirits, and with its evergreen leaves, this tree was thought to symbolize fertility and be an effective charm against witches and goblins.

EVERGREEN

FACT FILE

Height 8–15 m

Where Widespread; woodland, hedgerows, scrubland

Flowering April/May

Fruiting July

Leaf tint/fall Evergreen

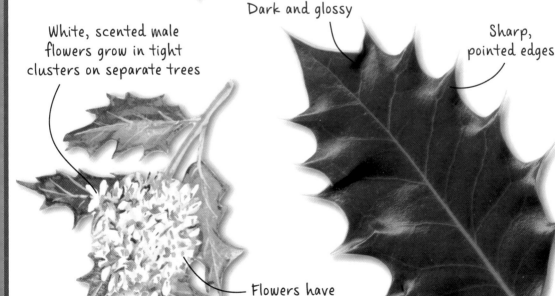

White female flowers grow near the base of leaves on female trees

Female flowers develop into shiny, red berries

Dark and glossy

Sharp, pointed edges

White, scented male flowers grow in tight clusters on separate trees

Flowers have four petals

MAGNOLIA
MAGNOLIA GRANDIFLORA

With their enormous, fragrant blooms and clusters of red seeds, magnolias are impressive trees. They originally came from the United States and are the state flowers of Mississippi and Louisiana. Magnolias are normally fertilized by beetles. Its petals are unusually tough, which minimises damage by the crawling insects. They are named after Pierre Magnol (1638–1715), a French botanist, and many different varieties have been cultivated.

EVERGREEN

Furry seed capsules (fruit) are up to 6 cm long and turn from green to orange-pink

Seed capsules open to release red seeds

FACT FILE

Height 12–25 m
Where Widespread; gardens, parks, arboretums
Flowering June–August
Fruiting September–December
Leaf tint/fall Evergreen

Thick and glossy with smooth edges

Six to twelve petals

Large, white, scented flowers up to 25 cm across

Up to 16 cm long

PEDUNCULATE OAK QUERCUS ROBUR

The pedunculate, or English, oak is known as the 'King of the forest' and it has a rich history, featuring in many myths and legends. English oaks provide a unique habitat for hundreds of species of other plants and animals. Oaks attract insects, which in turn attract birds, and acorns provide food for squirrels and other small mammals. A single tree can live for hundreds of years.

DECIDUOUS

FACT FILE

Height 15–25 m

Where Widespread; ancient woodland

Flowering May

Fruiting October

Leaf tint/fall November

Up to 3 cm long

Acorns (fruit) sit in cups at the end of long stalks, unlike the acorns of the sessile oak, which don't have stalks

Cluster of buds at the tip

Male catkins (flowers) are green-yellow

Three to six rounded lobes on each side

Almost no stalk

SEA BUCKTHORN
HIPPOPHAE RHAMNOIDES

This small deciduous shrub can be found growing on exposed, windy coastlines in salty conditions that few other trees can tolerate. Sea buckthorn is an increasingly popular plant that is cultivated for the extraordinary properties of its bright-orange berries and its deep and widespread roots. The berries are full of vitamin C and are used in skincare products. Its roots help to bind loose soil and add nitrogen to it, which is important for soil fertility.

DECIDUOUS

Male flowers are up to 4 mm across and grow on separate trees to the females

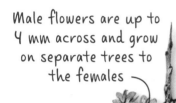

Green male flowers have leaf-like petals

FACT FILE

Height 1–3 m
Where Widespread; coastal areas, sand dunes
Flowering March/April
Fruiting September
Leaf tint/fall November

Fruits are bright-orange berries that grow on the female trees

Up to 8 mm long

Up to 6 cm long and 1 cm wide

Silvery-green, long and slender

Thorny, and develops silvery scales

SESSILE OAK QUERCUS PETRAEA

The sessile oak is one of just two native British oaks, but there are hundreds of different types in the northern hemisphere alone. The sessile oak is more likely to be found in stony uplands than the pedunculate oak, but they are similar in appearance. In Anglo-Saxon times, an oak was called an 'aik' and a seed was an 'aik-com', hence today's name – acorn. In one year, a mature oak tree produces as many as 50,000 acorns.

DECIDUOUS

FACT FILE

Height 15–30 m

Where Widespread; hillsides, woodland

Flowering April/May

Fruiting October/November

Leaf tint/fall November/ December

Orange-brown buds

Male catkins are yellow and drooping

Hard-shelled acorns (fruit) grow in clusters

Paler underneath with hairs on veins

Sessile acorns do not have stalks, unlike pedunculate acorns which have long stalks

Leaf stalks are 1 to 2 cm – much longer than those of the pedunculate oak

SPINDLE EUONYMUS EUROPAEUS

Spindles more often resemble bushes than trees, and they are often seen in hedgerows and woodlands. The timber of this plant was once used to make spindles – round, spinning pieces of wood that wool is wound onto. This gave the spindle tree its common name. The poisonous berries contain orange seeds that can be boiled to make a yellow dye. The berries have also been used in traditional remedies to cure farm animals of skin complaints.

DECIDUOUS

FACT FILE

Height Up to 5 m

Where England, Wales; hedgerows, woodland

Flowering May/June

Fruiting September/October

Leaf tint/fall October/November

Flowers grow in loose clusters

Flowers have four green-white petals

Long and oval-shaped with finely toothed edges

Green with shoots coming off at many angles

Each seed pod (fruit) is divided into four parts

Red seed pods open to release four small, orange seeds

Leaves turn orange and red in autumn

SWEET CHESTNUT CASTANEA SATIVA

These trees produce large, edible nuts that can be roasted and are often sold in streets, at fairs and other winter events. Sweet chestnuts have been long associated with winter festivals and were once seen as sources of magic. They are native to the warmer parts of Europe and were first brought to Britain by Roman soldiers, who relied on the nuts as an important part of their diet. Sweet chestnuts do not always ripen fully in Britain.

DECIDUOUS

FACT FILE

Height 20–30 m
Where Widespread; woodland, parks, well-drained soil
Flowering June/July
Fruiting October/November
Leaf tint/fall October–December

Long, male catkins (flowers) can grow as long as the leaves

Green, spiky female flowers grow at the base of the catkin

Sharply toothed edges

10 to 25 cm long

Tiny white dots, or warts, along twig

Fruits open to reveal one to three glossy, brown nuts

Spiky, green casing

The white willow grows well in damp soil and so is most likely to be found alongside streams and ponds, often near alder trees. Animals, especially horses, enjoy nibbling the leaves and tender shoots of this tree. The pale brown wood of the white willow burns easily and quickly. This tree can be pollarded every four or five years to produce a crop of straight poles, which are used for making fences.

DECIDUOUS

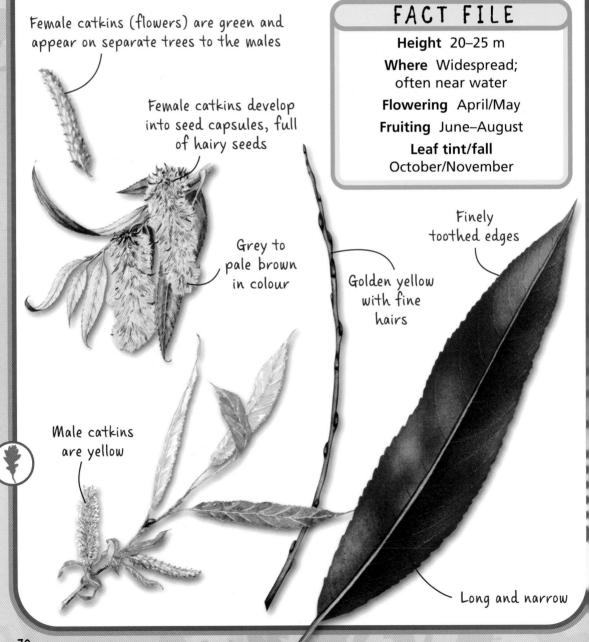

Female catkins (flowers) are green and appear on separate trees to the males

Female catkins develop into seed capsules, full of hairy seeds

Grey to pale brown in colour

Golden yellow with fine hairs

Finely toothed edges

Male catkins are yellow

Long and narrow

FACT FILE

Height 20–25 m

Where Widespread; often near water

Flowering April/May

Fruiting June–August

Leaf tint/fall October/November

FIELD MAPLE ACER CAMPESTRE

The field maple provides an ideal habitat for many small creatures, and plants such as lichens and mosses. Field maples are often found growing in hedgerows. In autumn, they can be identified by their leaves, which turn red and yellow. According to ancient myths, a child could be guaranteed a long life by being passed through the branches of a field maple. In some places, it was thought that field maples could protect a house against bats.

DECIDUOUS

White-green flowers have five petals

The wings are in a straight line, not curved as in the sycamore

Paired, winged fruits are like helicopter blades

Brown and coated in soft hairs

4 to 7 cm long, smaller than a sycamore

Three to five rounded lobes

FACT FILE

Height 8–14 m

Where Widespread; woodland, hedgerows

Flowering April

Fruiting June/July

Leaf tint/fall November

GUELDER ROSE
VIBURNUM OPULUS

Despite its name, this shrub is not a rose at all, but more closely related to the elder. Its unusual name comes from the Dutch province of Guelderland where it was grown as a decorative garden plant. Guelder rose berries are popular with birds, such as bullfinches, and small animals, but they are poisonous to humans. The berries can be used to make a red ink.

DECIDUOUS

Poisonous berries contain one seed each

FACT FILE

Height Up to 4 m
Where Widespread; woodland, scrubland, hedgerows, damp soil
Flowering June/July
Fruiting September
Leaf tint/fall October/November

Central flowers develop into red berries (fruit)

Buds grow in opposite pairs

8 cm long with three large lobes

Clusters of small, white flowers are encircled by larger flowers

Scented flowers have five petals

Leaves turn reddish-brown in autumn

HAWTHORN CRATAEGUS MONOGYNA

The hawthorn's leaves appear quickly in spring and its white blossom is a sign that summer is on its way. In folklore, in North Wales, Hawthorn was associated with death, possibly because the flowers' scent reminds some people of rotting flesh. However, the berries, leaves and flowers have been used in many past medicines. It also has long associations with May Day – its wood was used to make the first Maypoles.

DECIDUOUS

FACT FILE

Height 12–15 m
Where Widespread; hedgerows, scrubland
Flowering May/June
Fruiting March/April
Leaf tint/fall November

Small, white, scented flowers grow in clusters after the leaves have appeared

Stiff with brown buds

Long thorns up to 1.5 cm long

Deep red, oval-shaped fruits called haws

Haws contain one seed each, unlike those of the Midland hawthorn, which contain two

Dark green

Three to seven deep lobes

HORSE CHESTNUT
AESCULUS HIPPOCASTANUM

Horse chestnuts are best known for their glossy, brown nuts known as conkers. Competitors meet up in Northamptonshire every year to battle in the World Conker Championships – an event that has been running since 1965. Horse chestnut trees arrived in Britain in the 16th century and possibly get their name from the practice of feeding conkers to horses to cure them of illness.

DECIDUOUS

Upright spikes of white flowers

FACT FILE

Height 14–28 m

Where Widespread; woodland, parks, hedgerows

Flowering May

Fruiting September/October

Leaf tint/fall October/November

Flowers have five petals and a small pink spot near the centre

One brown nut, or conker, inside each spiky, green fruit

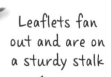

Sticky buds

Leaflets fan out and are on a sturdy stalk

Leaves are made up of five to seven long leaflets and appear in early spring

LONDON PLANE PLATANUS X HISPANICA

London plane trees are a familiar sight in many cities and towns. They were widely planted along streets in urban areas because they tolerate pollution. In the 17th century, American plane and oriental plane trees were cross-bred to produce this new variety. The London plane sheds dirt in its bark, which peels off through the year revealing a paler yellow bark beneath. Its attractive, hard-wearing timber is also known as 'lacewood'.

DECIDUOUS

FACT FILE

Height 13–35 m

Where Widespread; streets, parks, cities, towns

Flowering May/June

Fruiting September/October

Leaf tint/fall October/November

Male flowers are round and yellow

Female flowers are round and reddish

Lobes have triangular tips

Up to 25 cm long

Each spiky fruit contains many seeds

Many fruit cases stay on the tree throughout the winter

Green with smooth, pink buds

SYCAMORE ACER PSEUDOPLATANUS

In the autumn, sycamores produce thousands of spinning, winged fruits called 'keys'. The wings act like helicopter blades and spin the keys through the air so that they land some distance from the tree. The sycamore is also known as the martyrs' tree. In England in 1834, a group of workers – the Tolpuddle Martyrs – met under a sycamore to form a society to fight for better wages. They were expelled from the country as punishment.

DECIDUOUS

FACT FILE

Height 16–35 m

Where Widespread; woodland, hedgerows, mountains

Flowering April/May

Fruiting September

Leaf tint/fall October/November

Green buds grow in opposite pairs

Yellow-green flowers hang in spikes

Up to 15 cm long with five lobes

Each individual flower has five petals

Winged fruits, or keys, are green at first, then ripen to brown

Each key holds two seeds

Stalks are often red

WILD SERVICE TREE
SORBUS TORMINALIS

The wild service tree is an indicator of ancient woodland – areas where there has been continuous woodland since at least 1600. In spring, white blossom covers this tree and in autumn, its leaves turn coppery-red. Its berries, which were used to cure stomach upsets until the 1700s, are best eaten when overripe. This tree also goes by the name of 'chequers'. Some say this refers to the bark peeling off in squares and leaving a chequerboard effect.

DECIDUOUS

FACT FILE

Height 10–25 m
Where Southern England, Wales; ancient woodland
Flowering May/June
Fruiting September–November
Leaf tint/fall October/November

Stalks are hairy

Reddish-brown, berry-like fruits

Small white flowers hang in clusters on stalks

Green buds

Slightly glossy on upper surface

Up to 10 cm long

ASH FRAXINUS EXCELSIOR

The stately ash is one of the tallest deciduous trees in Europe and it grows easily in many habitats across Britain. In Scandinavian mythology, the ash was regarded as the tree of life. In English folklore, it was used to predict the weather. If oak buds opened before ash buds then the summer would be dry, but if ash buds opened first, the summer would be wet. The ash was once believed to provide defence against black magic and witchcraft.

DECIDUOUS

FACT FILE

Height 15–30 m

Where Widespread; woodland, hedgerows, hillsides

Flowering April

Fruiting June

Leaf tint/fall September/October

Winged fruits, called ash keys, hang in clusters

Some keys stay on the tree through winter, after the leaves have fallen

Toothed edges

Three to six pairs of leaflets with a single leaflet at the tip

Purplish clusters of flowers

Black buds

Flowers appear before leaves

ELDER SAMBUCUS NIGRA

The elder has proved to be a useful British tree, with the flowers, berries and stems all being put to good use. 'Elder' comes from the Anglo Saxon word *aeld* meaning 'fire'. The stems are hollow and were once used to blow air into fires. In Denmark, the tree was associated with magic and, before a tree could be cut down, permission had to be sought from its spirit. The flowers can be made into a cordial and the berries into wine.

DECIDUOUS

FACT FILE

Height Up to 10 m

Where Widespread; hedgerows, scrubland

Flowering June/July

Fruiting August/September

Leaf tint/fall October/November

Small, shiny, black berries (fruit) on red stalks

Heavy clusters hang downwards

Each tiny flower has three to five petals

Each leaflet is oval in shape

Soft and white in centre

Pale flowers have a sickly fragrance

Each stalk has two to four pairs of small leaflets with a single one at the tip

LABURNUM
LABURNUM ANAGYROIDES

A common sight in British gardens, laburnum is recognizable by its cascades of bright-yellow flowers in the summer. It originated in Europe and was introduced to Britain in the 16th century. All parts of the tree are poisonous, especially the seeds. The heartwood is deep brown in colour and was highly prized for making decorative items. It was often used as a substitute for the dark wood of the tropical ebony tree.

DECIDUOUS

FACT FILE

Height 6–9 m

Where Widespread; parks, gardens

Flowering May/June

Fruiting September/October

Leaf tint/fall October–December

Each hanging cluster of flowers is called a raceme

Long spikes covered in many yellow flowers

Seed pods (fruit) dry and open while still on the tree

Seed pods release black seeds that are very poisonous

Grey-green, with soft hairs when young

Each leaflet is oval

Each leaf is made up of three leaflets

ROWAN SORBUS AUCUPARIA

The magical rowan tree has a past steeped in history and mythology. 'Rowan' comes from the old Norse word for tree – *raun*. Its wood was used by Druids to make their staffs and magic wands. People used to put rowan sprigs in their houses to protect them from lightning, and sailors took it on board boats to ensure safe journeys. Raw berries are poisonous, but once cooked they can be eaten. They have also been used in herbal medicines.

DECIDUOUS

FACT FILE

Height 8–15 m
Where Widespread, mountains, parks, gardens
Flowering May
Fruiting October/November
Leaf tint/fall October/November

Small, creamy-coloured flowers grow in dense clusters

Each flower is 1 to 2 cm across

Leaves change to golden orange and reddish-brown in autumn

Each stalk has five to eight pairs of leaflets

Fruits are orange-red berries up to 1 cm long

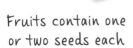

Fruits contain one or two seeds each

Purple-brown buds are covered in grey hairs

WALNUT JUGLANS REGIA

Walnut trees have been grown in Britain for their nuts, but also for their timber, which is one of the most beautiful woods in the world. There is evidence that walnuts have been growing in Britain since at least Roman times, and they were widely planted in the 1800s. Thousands of walnut trees were felled in the Napoleonic wars so that the timber could be used to make guns for soldiers.

DECIDUOUS

FACT FILE

Height 10–30 m

Where Southern England; woodland, parks

Flowering April–June

Fruiting September/October

Leaf tint/fall October/November

Female flowers are small and green

Male catkins (flowers) grow up to 15 cm long

Hollow inside

Fruits are round and green

Thick with a leathery surface

An edible nut is inside the tough outer casing

Five to nine leaflets

CEDAR OF LEBANON
CEDRUS LIBANI

This cedar is native to the mountain forests of the eastern Mediterranean, and has been a popular tree in parkland and large gardens in the UK. In ancient times, many of the cedar forests in Lebanon were felled for timber. Some stories tell of how this tree was first brought to Europe in the 18th century by a Frenchman, who uprooted a seedling while travelling in the Middle East. He stored the young tree in his hat, looking after it until his return to Paris.

EVERGREEN

Large seed cones (fruit) ripen to brown

Up to 15 cm long

FACT FILE

Height 8–35 m

Where Widespread; parks, large gardens, churchyards

Flowering June–September

Fruiting August–October

Leaf tint/fall Evergreen

Grey-green to yellow

Male cones (flowers) are up to 8 cm long

Needles are up to 3 cm long

Often in tufts

EUROPEAN LARCH LARIX DECIDUA

Larches grow tall and straight and, unusually for conifers, they lose their leaves in the autumn. These fast-growing trees produce good quality timber and they are often seen growing in plantations. In Siberia, it was once believed that man was created from a larch tree, and that woman was created separately from a conifer or fir tree. Herbalists use a weak tea made from the inner bark to treat stomach upsets and asthma.

DECIDUOUS

FACT FILE

Height 12–30 m

Where Widespread; woodland, parks, gardens, plantations

Flowering March/April

Fruiting September

Leaf tint/fall October/November

Reddish brown bark

Needles grow in bunches

Young needles

Seed cones (fruit) open to release seeds

Up to 3 cm long

Male flowers are soft, yellow cones

Female flower is pink-red

GIANT SEQUOIA
SEQUIOADENDRON GIGANTEUM

The giant sequoia is one of the tallest growing plants in the world and is also one of the longest living, capable of surviving up to 4000 years. The tallest specimen is the General Sherman in the United States, which, in 1987, measured 83.8 m tall. Giant sequoias come from California and were brought to Britain in 1853, the year that the Duke of Wellington died. This is how the tree got its other name – Wellingtonia.

EVERGREEN

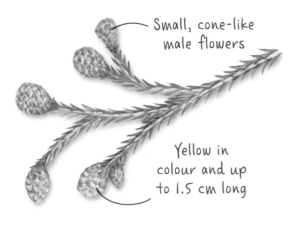

Small, cone-like male flowers

Yellow in colour and up to 1.5 cm long

FACT FILE

Height 20–50 m
Where Widespread; parks, grounds of historic buildings
Flowering May/June
Fruiting All year
Leaf tint/fall Evergreen

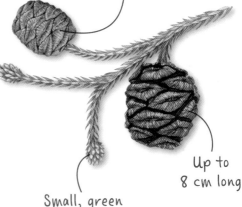

Young seed cones (fruit) are green, maturing to brown

Up to 8 cm long

Small, green female flowers at tips of shoots

Scale-like leaves

Scales are pointed and overlapping

JUNIPER
JUNIPERUS COMMUNIS

Juniper is a small, slow-growing, evergreen tree and can be found in a wide range of habitats all around the world. Its fruits can take two to three years to ripen, so black and green berries can be on the same tree. These are actually soft cones rather than true berries. As birds eat them and fly to other trees, they help distribute the seeds. In folklore, in parts of southwest England, the wood and needles were burned near a sick person and this was thought to cure infection.

EVERGREEN

FACT FILE

Height 5–10 m

Where Mainly southern England; woodland, scrubland, chalky soils

Flowering May/June

Fruiting All year

Leaf tint/fall Evergreen

Berry-like fruits take two to three years to ripen to black

Female flowers are tiny, green, scaly cones

Male flowers are small, yellow cones

Up to 8 mm long

Shoots are covered with slender, pointed needles

Needles grow in groups, or whorls, of three

NORWAY SPRUCE _PICEA ABIES_

It is believed that the Norway spruce was growing in Britain long before the last Ice Age. This species did not return to Britain until around the 1500s when it was brought over from Europe. It is grown in plantations for timber and also for use as Christmas trees. The German tradition of decorating Christmas trees became fashionable in England in the 19th century after Queen Victoria married the German nobleman, Prince Albert.

EVERGREEN

FACT FILE

Height 18–40 m

Where Widespread; plantations, parks

Flowering May

Fruiting September–November

Leaf tint/fall Evergreen

Female flowers are reddish-brown and darken with age

Mature seed cones (fruit) are up to 17 cm long and hold many small seeds

Small male cones (flowers) grow close to the ends of shoots

Reddish male cones turn yellow when pollen is produced

Rough and scaly

Short, stiff needles grow in a spiral pattern

SCOTS PINE PINUS SYLVESTRIS

There are many conifers growing in Britain today, but the Scots pine is native to parts of Scotland, making it the only native British pine. These fast-growing trees are found from Spain to Siberia. Scots pines grow tall and straight, and the wood is very hard-wearing, which makes it ideal for use as telegraph poles. The cones have been used to forecast weather – it is thought that when the cones open the air is dry, so no rain should be expected.

EVERGREEN

FACT FILE

Height 12–36 m
Where Widespread; woodland, plantations
Flowering April
Fruiting April
Leaf tint/fall Evergreen

Seed cones (fruit) are green at first, taking two years to ripen

Red female flowers grown in pairs

Long, slender needles up to 8 cm long

Mature seed cones are woody and up to 7 cm long

Needles grow in pairs

Small, yellow male cones (flowers) grow in groups

YEW TAXUS BACCATA

The dark, mysterious yew tree has been the subject of myths and legends for centuries, and it can often be found in cemeteries and church grounds. Known to live for hundreds – sometimes thousands – of years, several churchyard yews are more than 1000 years old. In ancient times, people planted yews where they would be buried. Most parts of a yew tree are extremely poisonous to humans and animals.

EVERGREEN

Fruits are red,
berry-like fruits,
called arils

FACT FILE

Height 4–20 m
Where Widespread; churchyards, woodland
Flowering March/April
Fruiting October
Leaf tint/fall Evergreen

Female flowers are
tiny, green cones
1 to 2 mm long

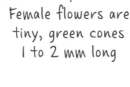

Small male flowers
turn yellow when they
release pollen

Male flowers sit at
the bases of leaves

Needle-like
leaves

Narrow, flat
and dark green

GLOSSARY

Bark The tough, protective outer layer that covers a tree's roots, trunk and branches.

Bough A main branch of a tree.

Bract A leaf-like part of a plant, found underneath a flower or its stalk.

Bud A rounded, undeveloped leaf or flower, often at the end of a twig or shoot.

Catkin A long, often hanging cluster of tiny flowers, on trees such as willows, oaks and birches.

Compound leaf A leaf made up of several smaller leaves called leaflets.

Coppice To cut back the stems of a tree to near ground level, causing many long, new shoots to grow up.

Cultivate To grow especially.

Deciduous Trees that drop their leaves every autumn.

Evergreen Trees that keep their leaves all year round.

Fruit The hard, soft or fleshy covering of the seed of flowering plants and trees.

Germinate To start to grow.

Girth The measurement around something, such as a tree trunk.

Hybrid A tree that is the offspring of two similar tree species eg the common lime.

Keys The dry winged fruits of ash, sycamore and maple, which often hang in a cluster like a bunch of keys.

Larva The worm-like young of an insect, eg a caterpillar, that changes into a winged, flying adult.

Leaflet A leaf or leaf-like section of a compound leaf.

Lobe A rounded part of a leaf that sticks out.

Native Originally from a particular country.

Nut A fruit that has a hard outer shell containing an edible kernel.

Phloem Tiny tubes inside plants that carry sugary sap up and down to all parts of a plant.

Photosynthesis The process by which green plants use the Sun's energy to turn carbon dioxide and water into the sugars a plant needs to grow.

Pollard To cut back the top branches of a tree to encourage more to grow.

Scrubland An area of land, often covered with shrubs, bushes and grassland.

Shoot A new growth of a plant.

Xylem A system of fine veins inside plants, made up of columns of dead cells joined together, which transport water from the roots to the leaves.